LEARNING UNLIMITED

Contents

Foreword

This is one of a series of papers published by Learning Unlimited, and now collected under the general title, 'The Learning Teacher'. It continues the original purpose which is to keep teachers up-to-date with what we know about how children and young people learn and how effective teachers teach.

A doctor who failed to keep up-to-date with medical developments over the past twenty years would have a quiet surgery. Yet in education, many teachers have now been in post for longer than that without receiving similar opportunities to update their knowledge about learning and teaching.

These papers summarise our best understandings to date about how we learn and how best to help other people learn. We still have a lot to discover but our knowledge is rapidly growing thanks to advances in neurology, psychology and, not least, good classroom practice.

At the end of a busy day, most teachers have neither the time nor energy to read lengthy academic texts. So the papers in The Learning Teacher series are short, readable and comprehensive: they 'do the reading for you' and those with particularly enquiring minds are directed to further reading at the end.

This is one of three closely related titles in this series. The other two titles are 'Teaching for Understanding' and 'Fostering Creativity - A Hard Look at Soft Thinking'. Each of these titles explores a key aspect of learning, namely understanding, thinking and creativity, looking at what we mean by the concept and making a case for its importance in learning, in school and in life. All three titles examine the difficulty of promoting understanding, thinking and creativity in schools as they are today and identify practical strategies and ideas for doing this more effectively.

'Teaching for Understanding' and 'Learning to Think' are particularly closely related topics. This title focuses mainly on strategies and ideas to help teachers to teach students to develop their capacity to think mainly outwith the existing curriculum. 'Teaching for Understanding' looks at how we can help students to learn more effectively in their normal class-work by teaching more consciously and consistently for understanding.

Here we will look at why thinking is important both in and out of school. We will identify different kinds of thinking and look at the difficulties of promoting thinking generally in schools. In doing this, we will touch on all the key questions that teachers ask about thinking in workshops:

* **Why is being able to think so important?**
* **How do children think?**
* **Are there such things as thinking skills? can they be learned or are they inherited?**
* **To what extent is the ability to think dependent on age?**
* **Are there different kinds of thinking for different areas of learning?**
* **Should teaching thinking have its own discrete area?**
* **What kinds of strategies and activities help children to think?**

I am grateful to Margaret Martin for giving me comments on an early draft of this title. My thanks also to Eric Young for the excellent job he did in editing and to Liz Callaghan for overseeing its publication.

Ian Smith, January 2006

Introduction: a thinking skills movement

thinking: a process of cognition, knowing, remembering, perceiving and attending. *The Concise Oxford Dictionary*

thinking skills: most lists include all or most of the following – absorbing information, analysing, drawing conclusions, brainstorming, problem-solving, evaluating options, planning, decision-making and reflecting.

Carol McGuinness (1999)

A central feature of education over the past forty years has been the development of what can only be called a thinking skills 'movement'. It has happened in response to the growing realisation that, as David Perkins (1992) put it, 'learning is a consequence of thinking' and that, traditionally, schools have not been all that successful at helping students to think.

Teaching thinking has been championed by a range of people, the best known of which are Reuven Fuerstein, Walter Lipman, Edward De Bono and Tony Buzan. Some, like Feurstein and Lipman, have focused their energies and efforts mainly on the school system while others have worked in the business and domestic markets. Some, notably Edward De Bono (who has written 62 books on the topic) and Tony Buzan, have been very successful commercially and their books fill bookshop shelves.

Teaching thinking has become a huge industry with several companies offering their own thinking workshops, programmes and training packages. Some offer schemes of work often in specific subject areas, but most tend to focus on thinking tools (Tony Buzan, for example, holds copyright on the term 'mindmapping') or specific programmes. Some you can simply buy off-the-shelf, others are more protected and are only made available through registered and trained trainers (this has been Fuerstein's approach). Focus 3 briefly describes the best known work on thinking skills undertaken in the past 30 years.

Some programmes are more recent, accessible and available than others. Some are backed by research evidence; many are not. In recent years, various surveys into thinking skills programmes have been carried out. They have looked at

available programmes, described them and the thinking on which they are based and reviewed any research into their effectiveness. In 1990, Nisbet and Davies looked at over 30 programmes out of over a hundred in the USA alone. Recent surveys in the UK have been carried out by Carol McGuinness on behalf of the DfEE in 1998 and by the Scottish Council for Research in Education on behalf of the Scottish Executive in 1999. A browse of the web will reveal further surveys carried out across the world and particularly in the US, drawing on hundreds of research documents and research reviews.

Despite all of this activity, there is still no clear answer to three fundamental questions about teaching thinking:

- What are thinking skills?
- How are they best taught?
- Do existing programmes actually work?

These are all questions we shall address in this paper before we move onto looking at the implications for school managers and classroom teachers. But we start with the rationale for teaching thinking.

1. Better grades, better citizens and beyond

"What is school for if it is not to help you to think and become a better person."

David aged 9, quoted by Robert Fisher in 'Teaching Thinking'

On one level, the question 'why is thinking important/desirable?' seems ridiculous. As human beings, we cannot not think. During the average day, we are reckoned to have about 60,000 thoughts. The real question is why is quality thinking or what has come to be known as higher-order-thinking so important in our schools, our society and the modern world generally?

'I think therefore I am'

The search for meaning is innate. Thinking is an essential part of what it is to be a human being. Other animals can think but humans' ability to perform higher-order-thinking is what sets us apart. The cerebral cortex, by far the biggest part of the modern human brain, is an immensely powerful meaning-maker desperate to make sense of the world. Young humans are mastery learners, naturally inquisitive and driven to make sense of the world, to work things out through touching, moving, tasting, smelling, looking, listening, thinking and asking questions.

"You can raise standards substantially only by improving the quality of thinking."

Philip Adey and Michael Shayler (1994)

Raising standards in school

It has been claimed that focusing on thinking skills can lead to better learning and increased attainment through fostering genuine understanding, information transfer and retention. It helps pupils to engage with what they are learning, to make meanings and impose structure. It helps them to understand, to solve problems and express their points of view effectively. It can help to move students' thinking up a gear. Research also shows that pupils are better motivated and more engaged in classes where they find intellectual stimulation.

Making teaching a more fulfilling job

Teachers often complain that their students can't or won't get involved in higher-order-thinking. They don't expect their students to think and feel obliged to do the thinking for them. As a result, students become bored and switch off or become totally dependent on the teacher. Ironically, what teachers most want is for their students to take more responsibility for their own learning and thinking. This would make the teacher's job much more rewarding and perhaps even a bit less demanding.

A successful society

Fisher (1995) argues that a successful society will be a thinking society. There is a growing realisation that, to be effective citizens and happy people in a world which is constantly changing, ever more complex and full of hype and spin, we need to be not just knowledgeable and skilled in some basic areas, but lifelong learners, able to think for ourselves. The ability to think effectively is critically important if we are to have a deeper understanding of the ideas and issues that affect our lives and be able to take good decisions on a daily basis. Democratic liberty depends on citizens having the skills to differentiate lies from truth.

2. Can't think, won't think, don't need to

"**Most people want to think**: they want to argue and converse about issues that are important to them such as what is going on around them and inside them. The problem is that our schools and our society as a whole encourages mindlessness." *Phillip Schlechty (1991)*

"We have a society that is full of examples of poor and inappropriate thinking at all levels." *Edward de Bono (1997)*

If our brains are indeed hard wired to think, if the case for thinking in the modern world is so strong, and if, as is argued, most people want to think, why do we have so many examples of 'sad' thinking (see Focus 1) in society, schools and classrooms? Before we answer that question, however, let's practice what we preach and examine the truth of the underlying assertion. There is plenty of evidence to back it up and it comes from a range of sources from the thinking skills 'gurus' like Edward De Bono to the vast majority of classroom teachers.

The intelligence trap

Over many years now, Edward De Bono has been the most cogent critic of poor thinking in our society. He argues that we take bad decisions all the time, based on very little or very poor thinking. Many of us don't feel the need or feel able to understand so many things that affect our lives and opt out of trying to do so. Good thinkers are considered to be people who are good at criticising others and proving them wrong. We are obsessed with simple solutions and 'either or', 'black and white' thinking. This is true at all levels and politicians are perhaps the best example. They fall into what de Bono calls the 'intelligence trap' more often than most. He points out that we mistake fluency in argument for thinking skills. As a result, many intelligent minds are trapped in poor ideas because they can defend them so well.

Mindlessness in schools

Why are teachers faced daily with students who use a range of tactics which are often (though not always) designed explicitly to avoid thinking? Guy Claxton (1999) has described these tactics in the terms set out below and, having discussed these

strategies with thousands of teachers over a number of years, I know that they ring very true to the vast majority of them:

1. Becoming invisible

Head down, merge into the background, avoid attracting attention

2. Going stupid

Say "I can't" - "I don't get it" - "don't ask me to think" - "just tell me the answer"

3. Being disruptive

Mess about, challenge the teacher, badmouth each other

4. Avoiding trying

It's better to be thought of as lazy than stupid, if you try and fail you must be thick

5. Refusing to engage

"This is boring" - "what's the point in this?" "I don't care" - "I hate history"

2. Can't think, won't think, don't need to

WHAT CONSTITUTES
'smart' and 'sad'
THINKING?

Focus 1

'Smart' and 'Sad' Thinking

Help young people to be able to spot good and bad thinking, both in themselves and in others. Talk to your pupils about what constitutes smart and sad thinking out in the real world. Select from and adapt the ideas on this handout to help you. Point out that everyone is a sad thinker at times, including you, and encourage them to pick you up when you slip into sad thinking. Even very clever people in academic terms can be sad thinkers: they make up their minds quickly and then use all their cleverness to defend what they think despite the evidence. As De Bono (1982) says, it's easy to criticise and analyse but much more difficult to create. Our egos are tied up with being right. But, in real life, right answers are few and far between. We need to tolerate ambiguity. You won't have to look far in the press, on television, in adverts or in the speeches of politicians for lots of examples of sad thinking.

Seven ways to be a 'sad' thinker

- Insist that what you think is true no matter what

- Only pay attention to things that support what you think and ignore everything else

- Always be certain: jump to conclusions as soon as possible

- Have all the answers: never admit you don't know

- Don't change your mind in the light of experience

- Use words like 'must', 'should', 'can't' and 'all', 'every', 'nobody' and 'never' as often as you can

- Avoid curiosity: stick to as few interests as possible: never go anywhere new or do anything different

Seven ways to be a smart thinker

- Admit that what you think now is only your best guess for the present

- Always be on the lookout for better ideas

- Don't feel you need to be certain all the time: avoid jumping to conclusions quickly

- Never be afraid to say you don't know: ask good questions

- Be prepared to change your mind

- When people use words like 'must', 'should', 'can't', 'every', 'nobody', 'never', ask yourself 'who says?', 'why not?', 'what would happen if?' and 'are there no exceptions?'

- Be curious: have a wide range of interests: go different places

3. Why is there so much 'sad' thinking around?

"Thinking is recognised as being one of the most tiring activities known to man, which presumably accounts for so few doing much of it for themselves." *Watt Nicoll (1998)*

Smart thinking is hard work

In many ways, higher-order thinking is just like hard physical exercise. While the latter is about pushing your body hard and developing your muscles, the former is about exercising your brain, pushing it hard and developing your learning muscles. Higher-order thinking is difficult: it means getting out of your comfort zone to challenge your own assumptions and to tackle problems that are not easily solvable. It means coping with what the psychologists call 'cognitive dissonance', or put simply struggling to understand. It literally involves growing new connections or different connections in your head. You need to be mentally and physically fit to do it and you normally cannot think at a high level for a long period of time without having a rest or time out.

Thinking requires will as well as skill

Because smart thinking is hard, you need to be motivated to do it. You need to want to do it, to believe that you can do it and have the self-confidence to try. A lot of people lack that confidence. As it gets increasingly complicated, modern life is full of everyday problems, many of which are complex without single correct solutions. Most people want simple clear-cut answers and do not have the confidence to deal with ambiguity. As a result, many people opt out, either denying that a problem exists in the first place or letting other people do their thinking for them, sticking to their normal routines and their set prejudices so that they have to think and learn as little as possible.

Thinking is often not nurtured from an early age

We are not born with fully developed higher order thinking skills, but infants and young children have abundant motivation to think. They are full of curiosity, desperate to explore the world and make sense of it, and of course brimming with questions for adults. In responding to these questions, adults can mediate children's learning and affirm the importance of asking questions and thinking things through. Children's curiosity needs to be nurtured, supported and developed, but often the opposite happens: adults become irritated by questions like 'why is the sky blue?' and make up an answer or say they don't know instead of helping them to think things through.

The traditional school system is responsible for a number of damaging myths about thinking in our society

In the past, the school system was based on the assumption that it was neither possible or necessary to teach thinking. This arose from an underlying assumption that thinking is a matter of intelligence which is something you are born with and cannot change (see 'Changing Our Minds About Intelligence') So, if someone is bright, they don't need to be taught to think and, if someone is not bright, there is no point. As a result, schools traditionally presented knowledge without promoting understanding (see 'Teaching for Understanding'). Also, schools focused almost exclusively on analytical or academic thinking and played down other kinds of thinking. Because of their experiences at school, many adults do not consider themselves to be capable thinkers. The school system has been changing only very slowly over the past thirty years.

Focus 2

Take young children's questions seriously

"We believe that the single most important thing that parents and teachers can do to help children develop their intelligence is a simple one: take children's questions seriously and turn these questions into opportunities to think and learn."

Robert Sternberg and Louise Spear-Swerling (1996)

The ability to ask good questions and to know how to answer them is an essential part of intelligence and it is a skill that can be learned – and lost. Children are natural question-askers, they have to be to grow up in a complex and changing environment. But whether they continue to ask questions, especially to ask good questions, depends to a large extent on how adults respond to their questions.

Sternberg and Spear-Swerling identify that, at the lower levels of response, adults can become irritated or dismissive and admit they don't know the answer or give the child information which may not be correct. At higher levels, they will mediate the child's thinking by, for instance, talking about possible explanations or working out answers together. Robert Fisher (1990) points out that, if adults simply operate at the lower levels of response, a damaging change often happens around the age of three or four which can last a lifetime:

The child learns to stop guessing and inventing answers when his efforts are rejected. After many rejections the child stops speculating. Instead he asks questions like, Daddy what is that? He learns that the answers lie not in what the child thinks but what the parent/teacher thinks. The focus of the learning passes subtly away from the learner to the teacher. If he does not know the right answer, he waits for others to explain.

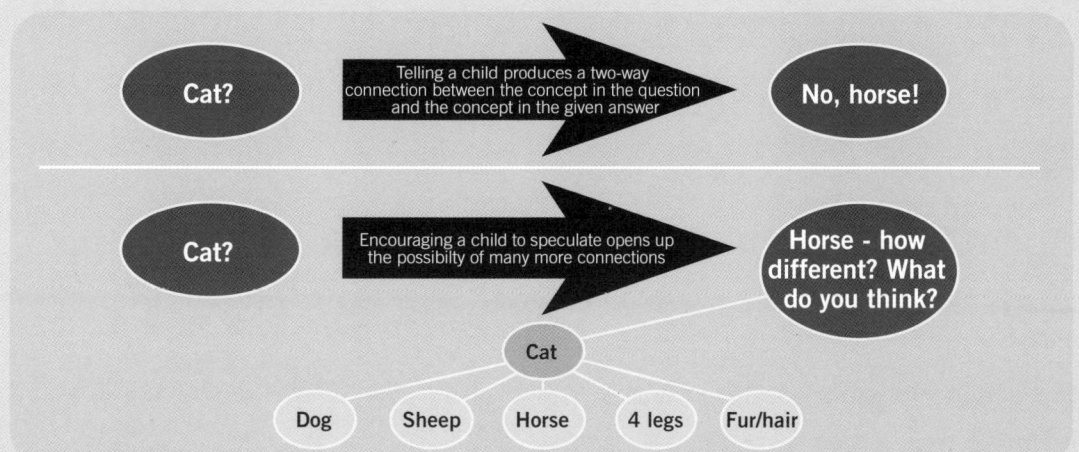

We would all like to think we always operate at the higher levels in how we respond to children, but probably only a most unusual parent or teacher does not occasionally lapse into doing this when tired and under stress. Usually adults 'tell' for the best motivations in the world. We have a strong innate desire to give young people the benefit of our knowledge and experience and of course there are many occasions when it is quite appropriate to do so and the child will be frustrated if you do not give them a straight and immediate answer.

4. Where does the idea of teaching thinking come from?

The idea of teaching thinking is by no means new. Improving the quality of thinking has been a central aim of education since the time of the ancient Greeks. Indeed the Socratic tradition lives on and is explicitly promoted through the 'Philosophical Enquiry' approach championed by Walter Lipman, which has become influential in many schools in recent years (see Focus 3).

Theories of learning

In modern times it's possible to trace the interest in thinking back to John Dewey and the publication of his book 'How We Think' in 1933. Dewey was the forerunner of a movement which led to the growth of cognitive psychology and the growing acceptance of constructivist views of learning as opposed to behaviourist and objectivist views. Piaget, Bruner and Vygotsky were all champions of constructivism. The thinking skills movement is based on a number of key assumptions not only about learning but about the nature of intelligence (see Changing our Minds about Intelligence).

The key assumptions on which thinking skills programmes are built

- Intelligence is changeable. It is a potential. The brain is like a muscle, which, if we don't use it, we lose it, and if we do, we can develop it

- Thinking is how we use our brains and develop their potential

- Most of our brains are underused and therefore capable of further development by stimulation: we can become better thinkers

- Learning is a consequence of thinking: we learn best when we actively make sense of what we are learning and relate it to what we already know

- We can intervene to help others develop or enrich their brains through higher order thinking. This can be taught

- Enhanced brain power or thinking skills will transfer across a range of subjects and contexts

"In my experience most schools do not teach thinking at all." *Edward De Bono (1992)*

"Education must be transformed to make thinking rather than knowledge its guiding priority." *Walter Lipman (1980)*

Dissatisfaction with the education system

I ended section three with forthright criticism of the effect our school system has had on our ability and confidence to engage in higher order thinking. Like De Bono and Lipman, many people believe that our education system was failing to teach pupils to think and that thinking rather than knowledge should be the top priority in schools. Mainly because of these kinds of concerns, the thinking skills movement has developed over the past forty years on both sides of the Atlantic and we will now turn to a description of that movement.

Focus 3

Thinking Skills Programmes

Over the past 20 years there has been a proliferation of thinking skills courses and programmes. These are some of the best known and widest used in UK.

Instrumental Enrichment

This is perhaps the best known example of a thinking skills programme developed by the world-famous Israeli psychologist 40 years ago to help adolescents with learning difficulties. It is a context-free cognitive development programme based on the concept of 'mediated learning'. An adult shows a learner specific methods for interpreting information and problem-solving. These become progressively more demanding through 14 instruments used over 2-3 years, introducing such concepts as syllogisms. Many of the extensive evaluations of IE show positive effects primarily on measures of non-verbal reasoning. Others show the main gains were in confidence and self-esteem.

Reuven Fuerstein

The Somerset Thinking Skills Course

This is a UK elaboration of the Instrumental Enrichment. It was developed as a result of dissatisfaction with the IE materials and a failure to demonstrate positive effects of IE in the UK. The programme consists of a handbook and six modules on topics such as problem solving and understanding analogies. The exercises may be used as a free-standing programme or integrated with the curriculum in upper primary or lower secondary. Unlike IE which presents abstract concepts, the Somerset course is pictorial and naturalistic. Evaluations have shown positive effects on a range of cognitive and related outcomes.

Nigel Blagg et al

CoRT Thinking

Edward de Bono has written over 60 books on teaching thinking. His brainstorming techniques and his 'thinking hats' (1985) are used in many schools. He has also developed a 2 year programme that aims to teach students of all abilities to apply their intelligence to any academic, personal or social situation. It consists of six sections, each of ten lessons including a teacher's handbook and lesson notes for pupils. An intensive study on CoRT in 1989 highlighted improvements in self-esteem as well as large gains in language arts and social sciences. It has been criticised for being too teacher directed and not dealing with the cognitive domain effectively enough.

Edward de Bono

Cognitive Acceleration in Science and Mathematics Education (CASE and CAME)

CASE and CAME, though set within the context of Science and Mathematics for 11-14 year olds, are structured programmes rather than the infusion method. They are designed as a series of one-hour inserts into existing courses. Unlike philosophy, which makes use of deductive reasoning (arguing from the given to the specific), CASE and CAME are based on inductive reasoning. They encourage children to move from concrete examples to abstract generalisations, noting dissonance and promoting bridging to other subject areas. They are among the most successful and well-evaluated thinking skills programmes and are directed towards scientific and mathematical thinking for 11-14 year olds.

Philosophy for Children

Lipman believed that children were 'natural philosophers' constantly seeking answers to questions. Teachers should model dialogue and structure classroom activities in ways that promote its self development, often using novels, stories and poems as stimulus material. The approach can be used across the curriculum particularly in the context of social and moral education. Evaluations show positive effects along many dimensions other than standard achievement tests. Robert Fisher has developed Lipman's approach in the UK by focusing on questioning within classrooms and the ways in which teachers manage the process to develop a 'community of enquiry'.

Matthew Lipman, then Robert Fisher

4. Where does the idea of teaching thinking come from?

Focus 3

Thinking through Geography

This is a series of books, the first of which was written about geography in 1998 by David Leat of the University of Newcastle. Since then a series of books have appeared focusing on thinking in different subjects including history and modern languages and all have the same rational and approach. They are designed around a set of 'big' concepts which the authors claim are necessary for an understanding of the subject. Exemplar lessons each of which targets a concept are developed. The lessons encourage the development of a vocabulary for talking about thinking and the use of talk and group work to generate and evaluate alternative solutions.

David Leat et al

Activating Children's Thinking Skills (ACTS)

This began as a project in the late 1990s to promote the development of thinking skills at key stage 2 in ordinary classrooms in Northern Ireland. A handbook was developed by the project leader, Dr Carol McGuinness from the School of Psychology at Queens University in Belfast and a small group of teachers using a strategy similar to the one adopted by David Leat (see above). Thinking diagrams or 'graphic organisers' were produced as an aid to making the steps in thinking explicit to learners. The project has been extended in Northern Ireland and is also being used elsewhere in the UK.

Dr Carol McGuinness

Let's Think!

This programme is designed to develop the thinking abilities of 5 and 6 year olds. It contains 30 activities which encourage pupils to recognise and develop the way in which they think. Let's Think! claims to improve children's ability to solve problems, enabling them to apply their enhanced thinking to all aspects of their learning. The different ways of thinking covered are: seriation, classification, time sequence, spatial perception, causality, and rules of a game. The materials are designed to be used by a teacher with a small group of pupils extracted from normal classwork over a 30 minute period. Each complete set contains a teacher's guide and pupil resource pack.

P. Adey, A. Robertson and G. Venville

A Guide to Better Thinking

This programme is aimed at 10-12 year olds. It emphasises higher order thinking skills with a focus on creative, critical and positive thinking while considering how to motivate pupils to want to use these skills. Though its aim is to support classroom use, the teacher's book draws upon a wide range of research into the teaching of thinking. The pupil's book contains activities in each of the three areas of thinking to complete as well as a review and award section. The activities are designed to be delivered as a series of separate lessons over the course of a term.

Anne Kite

(Some of these programmes are no longer readily available or accessible. I have given details of availability in the References and Further Reading section)

5. Teaching thinking – the key questions

"Trying to define thinking skills is impossible: the list is endless and it consists of nothing less than an inventory of the intellectual powers of mankind." *Walter Lipman (1983)*

The thinking skills movement is broad: it accommodates a wide range of views and opinions and debate still rages on over some fundamental questions.

What are thinking skills?

Lipman identified this as a problem some time ago and was not confident it could be solved. Some current experts recognise as many as thirty separate thinking skills. Carol McGuinness has suggested that some consensus is emerging as to what thinking skills are *(see page 3)*. Her list avoids vague terms such as 'critical thinking' and 'problem-solving' but includes 'brainstorming' which is now going out of fashion quite rapidly, because it is no longer considered to be particularly effective *(see Fostering Creativity)*

Most people assume that thinking skills are about higher order thinking. This may be easy to recognise: it's not routine, it tends to be complex, it encompasses multiple solutions, it can involve the application of multiple criteria which may conflict with each other, it involves uncertainty and it is hard work, involving considerable mental effort. However, this does not get us far in defining what it actually is and at what age it can be developed.

A major problem with definitions of thinking that has been highlighted by many in the thinking skills movement is that our society and our schools system has tended to put a great emphasis on and assign high status to analytical, intellectual or academic thinking. This is regarded as being most valuable, because it attracts increased earning power and status in the job market. Creative thinking has received much less emphasis. What Sternberg (1996) called practical thinking *(see Focus 4)* has been almost totally ignored. Another title in this series, 'Fostering Creativity and Ingenuity in Schools', will look specifically at these two kinds of thinking which are closely related to innovation and enterprise, two areas which society now wants to invest in.

In my view, the most serious flaw in the thinking skills movement has been the emphasis on the cognitive development over the affective. The message that feelings have nothing to do with thinking, indeed get in the way of thinking is a dangerous one. Some proponents of thinking skills have recognised this, notably Edward de Bono. In his view, emotion governs choices and decisions, not rationality. The critical issue is when to use feeling and emotion in the process, not whether. Too often we do so too early, rushing to judgement without using enough perception, without paying enough attention. For me, Carl Jung was well ahead of his time in recognising that feeling, like thinking, is a rational process and that in solving problems effectively, in taking decisions, in coming up with new ideas, both thinking and feeling have a role to play.

Taking all this into account and drawing on the work of Sternberg in particular I have offered a model of four kinds of thinking in Focus 4.

At what age can children learn to think?

This is another area for debate, which we look at in more detail in another title in the series ('Lessons from the Early Years'). Some in the thinking skills movement emphasise that thinking can be taught and learned at any age from birth until death. Robert Fisher (1995) says there are no magic thresholds, that it's ongoing and the sooner you start the better.

Other proponents of thinking skills still hold on to the idea of stages of development popularized by Piaget when the brain undergoes growth spurts. They reckon that these occur between the ages of 6 and 8 and again between 12 and 14. They believe that these are the key times for cognitive

5. Teaching thinking - the key questions

intervention to take place. They also argue that some thinking skills (involving abstract thought for example) cannot be acquired until the second stage of development. They also suggest that, when the brain reaches maturity around the age of 16, new thinking processes can become more difficult to acquire.

> "This book is not for you if you believe that thinking skills cannot be taught directly, but only by thinking about specific subjects or applying thinking in everyday life."
>
> *Edward De Bono (1992)*

Can thinking be taught?

The assumption that thinking can be taught is shared by everyone in the thinking skills movement. The key question has been what do we actually mean by this? There was a movement away from the idea of thinking being a thought process hidden in people's heads to the idea that it is a specific set of skills that can be learned and taught. De Bono's view expressed above illustrates this view at its most extreme, but as you will see from the table below most thinking skills programmes have subscribed to the view that thinking can be taught to some extent at least separately.

from teaching skills...

- Thinking is about having a set of skills, tools or techniques

- These tools and techniques can be taught and learned directly

- Thinking skills can be learned out of context: they do not need to be developed in subjects or in everyday settings

- Once you have learned these skills you can use them to think more effectively about anything: transfer from one situation or subject to another is automatic

...to developing minds?

- Thinking is best described as a range of mental processes

- These cannot be taught directly, but we can create an environment that will stimulate their development and help students to grow their capacity to learn

- Our capacity to learn grows when we apply our thinking in specific situations: thinking depends on the context and what we are thinking about

- The capacity we develop in one context can be applied in other contexts, but transfer does not normally just happen automatically

Recently, however, there has been a change of emphasis away from thinking being a set of specific skills that can be explicitly and separately taught to a set of mental processes that need to be developed. It has been pointed out that thinking skills are not like reading skills, numeracy skills or like riding a bicycle. Other terms such as thinking strategies, frames or habits of mind, thinking dispositions have also been used. Philip Adey (1994) prefers to talk about "accelerating cognitive development" rather than developing skills and suggests that the thinking skills in the national curriculum in England and Wales are not really skills but mental processes which cannot be taught directly, but that you can develop them in a learning environment which will stimulate their development. There certainly seems to be a move away from teaching skills to developing minds or as Guy Claxton (2002) puts it 'developing brainpower' or 'learnacy' as well as 'literacy' and 'numeracy'.

What is the best way to teach thinking?

Interestingly this somewhat academic debate about whether thinking is about skills or mental processes is mirrored by a much more practical debate, namely should thinking skills be taught separately or infused in to the curriculum? This is another fundamental question the answer to which leads to profound differences of opinion amongst teachers, developers and researchers. In this debate too views are changing.

The programmes to teach thinking vary widely and surveys have attempted to look at the similarities and differences and to classify them in some kind of way. Nisbet and Davies first identified 'separate programmes' and 'infusion' as the two main approaches in 1990 and most other researchers have stuck broadly with this two-way classification ever since. The table below summarises the difference and classifies the programmes in Focus 3. You will see from this that up to now the emphasis has been very much on separate programmes.

a separate subject...

Treat thinking as a specific subject or programme in its own right.

Most of the examples in Focus 3 take this approach, namely:

- Instrumental Enrichment
- Somerset Thinking Skills
- CoRT
- Let's Think
- A Guide to Better Thinking

Or deal with thinking in a separate series of lessons or inserts within a subject area.

Two of the examples in Focus 3 take this approach:

- Philosophy for children
- CASE and CAME

...or infused into the curriculum?

Embed the teaching of thinking within and across the curriculum as part of a whole school approach, with every member of staff involved

This route has been traditionally far less common, and really equates to the idea of teaching for understanding (see 'Teaching for Understanding' title)

Examples from Focus 3 are:

- Thinking skills in geography and other subjects
- ACTS

There has been strong support for the benefits of both types of programme, but research studies have shed very little light on which is best. There is no doubt that some students become adept thinkers with no explicit instruction at all. Some researchers have suggested that students whose out-of-school lives offer little experience of higher order thinking must be taught directly. But the big issue that those who favour this approach need to tackle is how far skills taught separately will transfer if they

will do that at all *(see Focus 6)*. There is a view that if skills are to be taught directly this should happen before they are applied within a subject area but that this needs to be followed by immediate application in the subject area and that explicit help needs to be given to facilitate that transfer.

Focus 4

Four kinds of thinking

There have been lots of attempts to categorise both thinking and intelligence into different types and levels. Howard Gardner's model of Multiple Intelligences (1983) has been the most popular and commonly known in recent years. I like Robert Sternberg and Louise Spear-Swerling's model which identified three kinds of thinking, namely analytical, practical and creative, to which I have added a fourth, namely emotional thinking, which owes a great deal to Daniel Goleman's (1995) concept of emotional intelligence. The main usefulness of this model for me is to broaden our thinking away from traditional academic or analytical thinking and also to make the point that thinking and feeling cannot be separated from each other and that all our thinking is underpinned by and dependent on our emotions.

Analytical thinking	Practical thinking	Creative thinking
• Analysing	• Practising	• Creating
• Judging	• Using	• Discovering
• Evaluating	• Applying	• Producing
• Comparing & contrasting	• Implementing	• Imagining
• Examining	• Innovating	• Supposing
Requires and develops:	**Requires and develops:**	**Requires and develops:**
Logic / understanding	Skills / expertise	Inventiveness / originality
• Eloquence	• Efficiency	• Imagination
• Inquisitiveness	• Realism	• Ingenuity
• Interpretation	• Proficiency	• Inspiration
• Logicality	• Skill	• Inventiveness
• Questioning	• Aptitude	• Originality
• Rationality	• Expertise	• Productiveness
• Studiousness	• Performance	• Stimulation
• Persuasiveness	• Know-how	• Intuition
• Thoughtfulness	• Experimentation	• Ambiguity tolerance

Emotional thinking

• Listening   • Respecting   • Empathising   • Accepting   • Challenging

Requires and develops: Character / values / dispositions

• Openness   • Optimism   • Enthusiasm   • Self awareness   • Love
• Hope   • Boldness   • Energy   • Humility   • Vision

Developed from: Robert Sternberg and Louise Spear-Swerling 'Teaching for Thinking'

6. Does teaching thinking work?

"Does teaching thinking improve results? It seems likely."

Steven Hastings TES May 23, 2003

This section highlights what seems to be a paradox. Namely that the thinking skills movement's influence appears to be growing, but there is still very little robust evidence that teaching thinking actually leads to improved results. It will then go on to seek to resolve the paradox and speculate on what the future might hold.

The idea of teaching thinking is growing in influence

Most of the time the thinking skills movement has operated on the fringes fired by the enthusiasm of a few dedicated devotees. It is in the areas of special needs and the gifted and talented it has perhaps been most influential. It has certainly not yet reached a mass audience in education. But there have been some signs that its influence is growing. As we have already noted reviews of research in thinking skills were undertaken in England and Wales and Scotland in 1999. In 2000 a 'Teaching Thinking' periodical and website were launched in the UK. In the first edition Michael Barber, Head of Standards and Effectiveness Unit at The DfEE and a key voice in Downing Street wrote an article where he argued that understanding and transforming the way in which children learn is crucial to raising standards.

The national curriculum in England and Wales now lists five higher-order skills pupils should develop: information processing, reasoning, enquiry, evaluation and creative thinking. In Scotland the official interest in thinking skills generated in 2000 has waned and although problem solving is listed as a core skill at all levels of learning and thinking skills from 5-16 little is done to promote thinking explicitly at national level.

But we have not proven that teaching thinking actually works

This is the biggest frustration about the whole issue of teaching thinking. If it's done well, then Steven Hastings is right to say it seems likely that it will work. But, despite the massive amount of research that has been done over the years to prove this, the verdict is still 'not proven'.

Hastings based his assertion on recent evidence on CASE (see Focus). Unlike a lot of studies this one was carried out over a reasonably long period of two years. It showed evidence that schools teaching CASE at key stage 3 go on to achieve 19% more A-C grades in GCSE science in England and Wales than similar control schools that use traditional methods. Significantly CASE students also achieved 16% more A-C's in English and 15% more in Maths suggesting that these students have successfully transferred their thinking skills into other subjects as well. But proponents of CASE have been disappointed that many people do not accept the research for a range of reasons, one being that it was carried out by the CASE team themselves who promote it and profit from its success.
Of course, no amount of evidence would be enough for some sceptics. But the charge of bias has been only one of the problems that research into teaching thinking has encountered. Despite the fact that several of the programmes have been well used over the years and a great deal of research has been gathered it is hard even for supporters of teaching thinking to argue that it is convincing.

For example, De Bono's CoRT thinking (see Focus 3) has been used by over 7 million students in 30 countries. Over the years a great deal of research has been done on the programme. An intensive study into CoRT in 1989 highlighted improvements in self esteem as well as large gains in language, arts and social sciences. Research also confirmed that skills were transferring into other subjects. But no-one has pulled the research on CoRT or thinking skills generally together in any systematic way. The research done in 1999 by McGuinness and SCRE were simply overviews of what research had been done rather than evaluations of the research that could provide definitive answers into what works.

6. Does teaching thinking work?

That would be impossible. There are so many thinking skills programmes and they vary so widely from each other by their very nature they are very difficult to assess. Even if you define the success of thinking skills programmes simply in terms of examination results and leave aside the other claims such as building self esteem and self confidence, improved classroom behaviour, helping young people be reflective, and rational and independent of thought, then it is remarkably difficult, time-consuming and expensive to prove.

Many of the studies are carried out under optimal conditions with teachers who are motivated for them to succeed. Most are of too small a scale, short-term, and generalisations are made from the findings. Even if you have control groups, you look for results over a considerable period of time and you run into huge difficulties of contamination by other factors which are impossible to control, for example the quality of teaching, the quality of the administrative support, the appropriateness of the programme to the students, the extent to which it was implemented in the approved manner and so on.

So what does the future hold for teaching thinking?

I believe the apparent paradox described above has arisen because the argument about the importance of thinking in learning has largely been won. But the argument for separate thinking courses has not, and probably won't ever be won to the satisfaction of most teachers, for two reasons:

- **There is not, and probably never will be sufficient proof that separate thinking skills programmes work:** it's hard, if not impossible, to prove that transfer occurs from these courses despite the huge number of attempts to do so. Certainly if explicit attention is not paid to transfer, then it is hard to see that it will necessarily simply just occur

- **Separate thinking skills programmes are too difficult to introduce and sustain in the existing set-up and climate in schools:** most separate programmes make considerable demands on the teacher in terms of skill and commitment. Also, teaching thinking through separate courses or separate inserts within existing courses is hard for managers to justify in a crowded curriculum and the time constraints in schools

It can also be argued that there is less of a need to teach thinking explicitly as over the past twenty years there has been a shift in emphasis from knowledge to understanding in the mainstream curriculum. Most curriculum and assessment systems across subject areas now stress the importance of teaching and assessing understanding *(see 'Teaching for Understanding')*. Perhaps the road ahead is to develop minds within and across curriculum areas. But in the meantime I think there is still a place for learning skills.

Focus 5

Does your teaching have transfer value?

"Give me a fish and I will eat today. Teach me to fish and I will eat for a lifetime." *Chinese Proverb*

What is transfer?

Transfer means learning something in one context and applying it in another. We learn to drive a particular car and then can drive another one. We learn a reading skill in English and apply it in social subjects. We learn French and can apply some ideas when later learning Italian. We learn to manage squabbles with our brother and can apply the same skills in managing social relations at work later in life. Any situation is a little different so all learning involves a little transfer. Real transfer occurs when people can carry something over that they learned in a significantly different context.

Why is transfer important in education?

We need plenty of transfer for education to have the impact we want. We don't teach reading so that you can read in the English class only. We want pupils to be able to use the knowledge they have learned in Maths in physics and in the supermarket for instance. If education does not achieve considerable transfer it's not worth much.

Why worry about transfer?

Some transfer happens automatically, but research shows that students do not spontaneously transfer nearly as much as we would like them to. Lots of the knowledge pupils gain in school is inert. It's there but it's passive and they don't know how to use it in different contexts. The moral is we need to teach for transfer.

When does transfer happen?

Some transfer happens automatically. This has been called 'near' or 'low-road transfer'. It usually happens when the new context has a lot of similarities to the one in which you learned, for example driving a van after learning to drive a car. Opening a chemistry book for the first time triggers reading habits acquired elsewhere. Interpreting a bar graph in geography automatically brings up mastering bar graph activity in Maths.

Some transfer does not happen automatically, however, because the similarity between the two contexts is much greater or may not appear to exist at all. This is sometimes called 'far' or 'high-road transfer'. It depends on deliberate mindful abstraction of a skill or knowledge from one context for application in another. Deliberate thought has to be given by the learner about whether and how skill or knowledge can be applied in another situation. This can be forward looking or backward looking.

How do we teach for transfer?

We can design our teaching to make the learning more likely to transfer in two ways. Firstly we can examine what we are teaching and focus on teaching topics or using examples which have transfer potential. If a topic or an example doesn't have transfer potential we should think of abandoning it in favour of one that has. Secondly we can look at how do we can teach for transfer more systematically and persistently - lots of teachers simply do it intuitively. We can make our instruction more like the contexts we want it to transfer to by teaching the knowledge in the context it will be used in (sometimes called 'hugging'). For instance if we want students to relate literature to their everyday lives you might choose texts where the connection is particularly plain (e.g. Romeo and Juliet rather than Macbeth). If this is not possible we can help students to make connections that require them to reflect (sometimes called bridging).

Main source: Robin Fogarty, David Perkins and John Barell 'Teach for Transfer'

7. Thinking, the way ahead

"The idea of thinking-as-a-skill still has theoretical and instructional force." *Carol McGuinness (1999)*

As thinking has come to be seen as more and more important, so the role that schools play in promoting thinking has come under greater scrutiny. Given the debates that have raged around teaching thinking and learning to think we have looked at in the last two sections it's hardly surprising that schools and teachers find it difficult to decide what is the best way ahead for them and their students.

Even if you take time out to read widely it's very hard to make sense of the current state-of-play in thinking about thinking. There are lots of programmes and support materials around, and there is a wide range of advice about, some of it conflicting. On the one hand there is a growing belief that students will not learn to think and how to learn simply by being taught science, maths or history and that students need to be taught explicitly to think and to learn. But on the other hand we are still not clear what thinking skills actually are and whether teaching thinking programmes separately from the main curriculum is effective.

This section and the ones that follow are an attempt to give school managers and teachers some guidelines for strategy and practice.

Advice for curriculum managers

I think the big challenge is to avoid the situation where students regard learning to think as something that happens at specific times and teachers regard teaching students to think as something that somebody else does somewhere else.

- Continue to encourage teachers to put a growing emphasis on teaching for understanding within subjects and curriculum areas. *(see Teaching for Understanding title)*
- Where can you foster links across subject areas and into real life situations? This will be easier in primary schools than secondary schools. In Scotland, at any rate, I predict a return to the out-of-favour topic approach to at least some degree
- Be careful not to see, or encourage our students to see, thinking simply as a skill that can be taught and learned out of context

and specifically to equate thinking simply with study skills that help students to perform in examinations
- But don't abandon the idea of teaching some thinking skills explicitly and separately - teachers with particular interests and expertise could be used to do this *(see examples below)*
- But it's crucial that they are applied and applied quickly in subjects and contexts and that all staff see it as their responsibility to teach thinking and promote the transfer of thinking skills into other subject areas and into real life situations
- Be aware that creating a climate for thinking and respect for other people's ideas is important in the staff room as well as the classroom

This example illustrates how the two different approaches to thinking skills can be reconciled in a practical way:

The headteacher of a secondary school was particularly keen to promote mindmapping. She worked with staff who were comfortable with the technique themselves to ensure that it was taught systematically to all students in their first year in secondary. Secondly she ensured that all staff were thoroughly briefed on mindmapping and what pupils had been taught. Some departments and teachers enthusiastically (the Head of History attended a Tony Buzan course on mindmapping) embraced the technique and gave students opportunities to use it regularly. Others were not so confident in teaching the technique themselves or building it into their own teaching. But their attitude was summed up by a Modern Language teacher who reported that she did not use the technique herself, but she was very happy for pupils to use it if they felt it helped them.

Advice for teachers

Let's be clear. Helping your students to learn to think is not easy in a school setting. It requires commitment, perseverance and skill. Here are five ways to do it, each of which is elaborated in forthcoming sections:

- First and foremost create a climate where there is respect for other people's ideas *(see section 8 and Focus 6)*
- Bring these ideas out through your questioning and your students' questions *(see section 9)*
- Teach for transfer - give your students explicit help to link what they are learning to what they have learned previously, to other aspects of the subject, to other subjects in school and to their lives generally *(see Focus 6)*
- See it as part of your job to help your students build a toolkit of learning techniques *(see section 10 and Focus 8)*
- Help your students to develop a learning vocabulary, encourage metacognition, in particular to decide which tools work for them and when *(see section 11)*

We think in different ways

I have made very little mention in this title about the fact that we all prefer to think in different ways and we have different strengths as thinkers. This is because we have dealt with this topic in detail in another title in the series *(Different in Similar Ways)*. This is a crucial message for everyone involved in supporting thinking. Some of the ways in which students think may help them to fit into the current school system. These are outlined below. It mirrors Focus 4 and like the information there is developed from Sternberg and Spear-Swerling.

Analytical thinkers may tend to fit into schools, they may:

- Get good marks and grades
- Be liked by teachers
- Feel accepted by school, follow directions
- Be good at evaluating other people's ideas
- Be natural critics
- Prefer to be given directions

Practical thinkers may not fit in well, they may:

- Get moderate to low marks and grades
- Be viewed as turned off by teachers
- Feel bored by school
- Like what they do to be relevant
- Like to apply ideas in a pragmatic fashion
- Have natural common sense
- Like to be in practical settings

Creative thinkers may not fit in well to schools, they may:

- Get moderate to low marks and grades
- Be viewed as a pain by teachers
- Feel confined by school
- Not like to follow directions
- Like to come up with their own ideas
- Be natural ideas people
- Like to self direct

In schools emotional thinkers may or may not fit in, they may:

- Get a wide range of grades
- Become the teacher's pet or the likeable rogue
- Feel out of place or put down in school
- Fit in when they feel appreciated
- Like what they do to fit their values
- Be good at seeing others' perspective
- Be good people persons
- Like to be in relationships where they feel valued

8. Establish respect for other people's ideas

Higher-order thinking is as much about will as it is about skill. It's hard and it's risky so it requires motivation and confidence. Students, especially in upper primary and secondary, usually have to be challenged or 'pressed' into higher-order thinking, but they also need to feel safe. A crucial factor is that they have to be sure that other people will have respect for their ideas, will support them when they express their half-formed understandings and will not ridicule their mistakes.

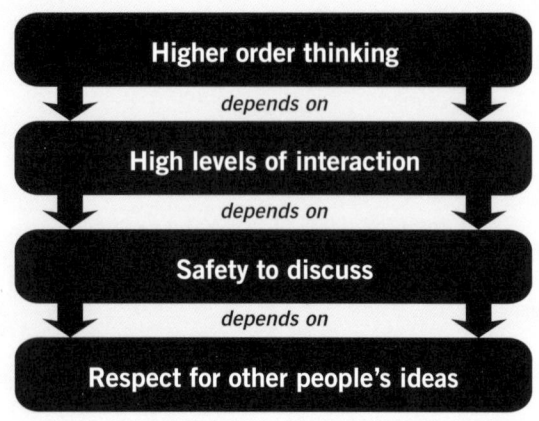

There is robust research to show that successful teachers all engage in above average levels of interaction in the classroom. As Galton and Simpson who carried out one of the largest research projects into progress and performance in primary classrooms in 1980 pointed out, this appears to be an important determinant of pupil progress.

The teacher can achieve these levels of interaction in a variety of ways. You don't have to favour group work as opposed to whole class teaching. You don't have to subscribe to a particular philosophy of education either be it pupil centred or teacher directed. You can do it by teaching from the front (being 'a sage-on-the-stage') or by coaching and facilitating (being a 'guide-on-the-side') but it is the level and quality of the interaction that seems to count. You certainly need to avoid being a 'bore-on-the-floor'.

Creating a climate where pupils feel safe to discuss is very difficult in many classrooms. It is not only the teacher that has to respect students' ideas but fellow students, as Magdalene Lampert (2001) points out:

"To create a climate in the classroom where pupils feel safe to question and discuss without being put down – where they can explore their half-formed understandings out loud is difficult in most schools. In many classrooms pupils whom everyone agrees are smart get to dominate discussions and others feel incapable of either judging or challenging their assertions. If students are to think and learn together, those considered by themselves and their peers to be of lower ability would need to be able to disagree with students considered to be smart. Conversely students of greater ability would need to respect the thinking of all students. To achieve this is not easy. It's about establishing and maintaining relationships and requires constant attention."

Focus 6 gives some suggestions about how to establish and maintain such relationships and what to give constant attention to.

Focus 6

Seven ways to create a climate for thinking

A thinking classroom is a stimulating environment, where there is relaxed alertness, high challenge but high support and low stress, where there is high energy, low tension. Establishing that and maintaining it is not easy. Indeed it is a balancing act. It's about asserting your authority, while at the same time helping young people take responsibility for their own behaviour and their own learning. It's about getting a grip and letting go. Teachers who manage to walk this tightrope successfully do it differently and indeed can be very different from each other. But this disguises how much they have in common.

1. **Get them to behave first:** Create order and a sense of security by modelling and teaching appropriate behaviour; establish rules and consequences; base the rules on clear values and apply them fairly; be assertive rather than passive or aggressive as consistently as you can.

2. **But from the very beginning build positive relationships:** Value and respect young people: listen: be an encouraging adult and use lots of positive affirmations: as time goes on share more of yourself - come out from behind your position and be a human being not just a teacher.

3. **Have high expectations of all students:** Believe that all young people can learn and communicate that belief to them. Press them to think – set up what is sometimes called 'cognitive conflict.' Keep the pace and level of lessons just above the average ability of the class. Challenging tasks motivate. Most teachers worry too much about the lower ability pupils and go too slow for the majority of the class. Some will drop off but others will get caught up in the slipstream and get pulled forward. The reality is that most classes are full of people not getting it first time round and pupils are more used to not getting it than you think.

4. **But avoid excess stress and tension:** Don't set unrealistically challenging tasks: we concentrate and perform best on tasks that are just beyond their current capabilities. Help students to maintain a state of relaxed alertness by banning threats, put-downs, backbiting and sarcasm and coming down hard on anyone who breaks this rule.

5. **Develop a questioning climate** in which students feel able to share their thinking and their ideas: where not only is there is no shame in getting things wrong, making mistakes, or being stuck but these are seen as things that good learners do on a regular basis.

6. **Encourage collaborative ways of working:** Play down competition and comparisons between individuals: have students working as pairs and groups regularly and use strategies like circle time; actively teach and model the skills needed to take part in quality discussions.

7. **Trust students and give them responsibility before you are sure they are ready:** Gradually help students to develop the attitudes and skills they need to take responsibility: ask their advice, be prepared to solve classroom problems with them and give them a real say in how they learn and what goes on in the classroom.

9. Ask hot questions

Fat and thin questions

One way to challenge students and get them thinking is to ask fewer and better questions and encouraging them to ask better questions. Better or 'fat' questions are ones that set up what has been called 'cognitive conflict' that provoke or lead to higher-order 'productive' thinking as opposed to lower order 'thin' questions that lead to 'reproductive' thinking. Teachers tend to ask a lot of thin 'guess-what-I-am-thinking' questions to which there is only one obvious right answer.

We looked at how to ask better questions in subject areas in *'Teaching for Understanding'* but there are generic higher-order thinking questions that can be asked across subject areas, such as the ones below.

Hot questions

- What do you think?
- Why do you think that?
- How do you know?
- Do you have a reason?
- Can you be sure?
- Is there another way?
- What do you think happens next?

It's also important to encourage students to ask better questions and to help them be aware of what constitutes better questions. The concept of fat and thin questions can help here. Even young children understand this concept. Fat questions are ones you have to think about, thin questions are ones to which there is only one obvious answer.

Levels of thinking and questioning

As well as the work that has been done on different kinds of thinking *(see section 5)*, there has been a lot of work done over the years to identify and describe different levels of thinking. The results of this work can help teachers to determine the level of questioning that is appropriate and to prepare and plan both individual questions and questioning strategies. There are lots of these 'taxonomies' about, but the most famous was produced in 1956 by a group of educators in the United States and has stood the test of time remarkably well.

Benjamin Bloom and his colleagues set out to classify cognitive, affective and psychomotor skills in 1948. It wasn't until 1956 that they were able to publish their taxonomy of cognitive skills and they never got round to the other two. Even the taxonomy's approach to the cognitive domain came into a fair amount of criticism as soon as it was published. He never claimed that kinds of thinking were separate from each other but the differences between some many people found hard to discern. Many did not like the fact that the taxonomy was hierarchical and did not agree with Bloom that you needed to master lower order thinking before you could move onto the higher realms. Also it was pointed out that metacognition had not been included. Others have set out to put all these failings to right since then but Bloom's taxonomy is still the most popular. We have found that teachers still find Bloom's list useful in devising higher- order cognitive questions. Our version of it with samples of questions from a range of subject areas is included in Focus 6.

ENCOURAGE YOUR LEARNERS TO ASK
hot questions!

Focus 7

Six levels of thinking

1. Knowledge (Know it)

Can take in various types of information and recall it when needed.

- Knows basic facts and can recall or state information, repeat them or give information about them
- Knows how to follow routine procedures

Cue words:

Repeat, list, record, name, relate, tell, show, label, collect, state.

Prompts:

What happened after...? How many...? Who was it that...? Who spoke to...? Find the meaning of... Which is true...?

Kinds of performance:

- Relate what happened in the story of Goldilocks and the Three Bears
- Tell me what kinds of weather do we get
- Say who wrote Hamlet
- Name the formula for the area of a circle
- State the first law of Newton

2. Comprehension (Understand it)

Can give meaning to information at a basic level.

- Goes beyond right answers to explaining why the answer is right or wrong
- Grasps the meaning of ideas, instructions and problems and can explain them in own words
- Can provide an explanation that makes sense of something that is difficult or puzzling
- Knows how/why something works, something is so, or something happened

Cue words:

Restate, discuss, describe, explain, recognise, express, identify, locate, report, operate, schedule, sketch.

Prompts:

Can you write in your own words...? What do you think...? What was the main idea of...? Can you distinguish between...? Can you provide an example of what you mean by...?

Kinds of performance:

- Recognise why Goldilocks liked the little bear's bed best
- Discuss why we need to know about the weather
- Describe what they think Hamlet meant when he said 'to be or not to be'?
- Express why 7 is a prime number
- Explain in your own words what it means to go at a constant speed in the same direction and what sorts of forces might divert the object

3. Application (Use it)

Can use a learned skill in a new situation.

- Uses existing information or know-how or skill in new situations or real life
- Makes inferences and anticipates probabilities
- Explains and interprets information and uses it to solve problems

Cue words:

Translate, interpret, apply, employ, use, demonstrate, dramatise, practise, illustrate, criticise, diagram, inspect, debate, inventory, question, relate, solve, examine, justify, generalise, predict, support, verify, prove, infer.

Prompts:

Do you know of an instance where...? Can you apply this method to some experience of your own? What facts would change if...? Would this information be useful if you had to...? Could this have happened in...?

Kinds of performance:

- Can say what they would have done if they were Goldilocks
- Can tell to what extent today's weather forecast was correct
- Can relate Hamlet to everyday life and to their own lives
- Can give fresh examples of Newton's law at work: for instance identify what forces divert the path of objects in sports, in steering cars, in walking

Focus 7   continued

4. Analysis (Examine it)

Can break down information into parts and relate the parts to the whole.

- Can describe what is happening (e.g. in a football game) and why; can distinguish between facts and opinions
- Can see patterns, organisation of parts, recognition of hidden meanings, identification of components
- Can recognise fallacies, relevance and irrelevance

Cue words:

Distinguish, analyse, differentiate, appraise, calculate, experiment, test, compare, contrast, create, design, setup, organise, manage, prepare.

Prompts:

How is this similar to... Which event could not have happened if... How was this similar to...? Why did...occur? What are some of the problems of...? What was the turning point in the story?

Kinds of performance:

- Say which part of the story of Goldilocks they liked best
- Be able to say how the weather affects us
- Distinguish the main themes in Hamlet
- Offer evidence in defence of Newton's law

5. Evaluation (Judge it)

Can make an objective judgement about the value of something based on a recognised standard.

- Can make generalisations, develop criteria, make decisions, judge accuracy of a statement or the merit of an idea
- Assess the value of theories, recognise subjectivity
- Make choices based on reasoned arguments
- Verify the value of the evidence

Cue words:

Judge, appraise, evaluate, rate, compare, value, revise, score, select.

Prompts:

Is there a better solution to...? Judge the value of... Defend your position about...

How would you feel if...? What changes would you recommend and why? What do you think about...? Why do you think that?

Kinds of performance:

- Be able to judge to what extent Goldilocks was bad or good and why
- Evaluate what they have learned about the weather
- Decide which of the two films you have seen of Hamlet is the best and why
- Explore the relationship of Newton's law to physics as a whole - why is it important?
- What role does it play?

6. Synthesis (Create it)

Can combine existing elements to create something new

- Builds a pattern or a structure from diverse elements
- Plan projects, form hypotheses, make predictions, communicate ideas
- Solves problems that don't require one single correct answer

Cue words:

Compose, plan, propose, predict, design, formulate, arrange, assemble, collect, construct, choose, assess, estimate, measure

Prompts:

Can you design a... to...? What is a possible solution to...? What would happen if...? Can you think of some new and unusual uses for...? How would you devise a way to...? Can you develop a proposal that would...?

Kinds of performance:

- Predict what they would have done if they were Goldilocks
- Compose a poem about the weather
- Say what Hamlet tells us about honour and loyalty?
- Formulate an experiment to test Newton's law: e.g. can you set up a situation as little influenced by gravity and friction as possible

10. Teach technique and develop know-how

Traditionally teachers have seen themselves as teaching know-what rather than know-how. That needs to change and is changing. Secondary schools in particular have recognised that raising achievement depends on helping students to develop their learning skills. There are lots of courses and materials on the market that explicitly set out to raise grades and examination performance through helping students to study, revise, memorise information and pass examinations. Many schools are also bringing outside experts in to work with students on these skills or are building these techniques into personal and social development programmes.

There are three potential problems with many study skills courses. The first is that many of them put the emphasis less on understanding and higher-order thinking and more on how to take in information, store it and recall it. The second is that transfer does not occur and pupils do not apply the skills in subject areas, and the third that teachers do not build on the techniques learned or may not even know what has been taught.

These problems can be overcome firstly if a school works to ensure that every teacher sees themselves as responsible for helping pupils to develop a toolkit of techniques *(see the example below)*. Secondly that toolkit includes a wide range of thinking techniques *(see Focus 8)* which are not simply used to help students cram for examinations.

Toolkit of techniques

- Classifying
- Keywording
- Relaxation
- Self-evaluation
- Focusing attention
- Positive thinking
- Team-working
- Problem solving
- Summarising
- Visual note-making
- Time management
- Critical thinking
- Mnemonics
- Goal setting

Teaching techniques such as mindmapping will not in themselves lead to higher-order thinking or develop minds if the tools are simply used to memorise information. But there need not be a tension between learning to study, passing exams and learning to think. We certainly need to help students move away from the study that is wasted on aimless, unfocused reading and indiscriminate copying from books. If the emphasis is put less on mnemonics and more on techniques that first and foremost help students to make learning more active, to use new information quickly, to do something with it and to keep thinking about it, to seek out the meaning and to structure it in a way that is relevant to them, then there is not a problem.

A very useful concept to share with students is the idea that as they go through school and life they should think of themselves as developing their own personal toolkit of thinking techniques which they can develop, refine and add to as they go along. The better your set of tools the smarter a thinker you will be; the smarter a thinker you are the better your tools are.

problem solving
team-working
positive thinking
focusing attention
self-evaluation
relaxation
keywording
classifying
summarising
visual note-making
critical thinking
mnemonics
goal setting

HELP PUPILS DEVELOP
a toolkit
of techniques.

Focus 8

Thinking techniques

There is a wide range of techniques to help learners focus attention to help with the three P's of perception, processing and presentation, which, by the way, don't necessarily happen in that order or at the same time.

Learning Involves

Perception:

• Getting ideas into our heads

Processing:

• Organising ideas in our heads

Presentation:

• Getting ideas out of our heads

De Bono is particularly strong on the importance of perception and I particularly like his range of tools to help people 'stop and think' such as PMI (Plus Minus and Interesting), CAF (Consider All Factors), APC (Alternatives, Possibilities, and Choices).

For processing I particularly like the work of Oliver Caviglioni and Ian Harris ('Mapwise') in helping students to keyword, classify and summarise information. I also like De Bono's thinking hats for helping learners to think about and process information in different ways. *(See Fostering Creativity – A Hard Look at Soft Thinking)*

For presenting ideas (and indeed for generating ideas and processing them as well) I particularly like the idea of visual organisers. Pride of place here needs to go to Tony Buzan who invented the term 'Mindmapping' and has done more than anyone over the past thirty years to popularise this technique. He did not invent the technique itself however and there are many, many other forms of visual organiser fifty of which are documented by Oliver Caviglioni and Ian Harris (Eye Cue).

Visual ways of helping students to think are particularly important and have been undervalued in the past. Using visual organisers is a skill that needs to be taught and also requires other skills (for instance if using concept maps to summarise a chapter in a book, pupils will need to be able to identify keywords). Representing your thinking visually can help you to get information out of your head onto paper (e.g. generating ideas, when planning a project, an experiment or a story), to get information into your head (e.g. when listening to someone talk, watching a video or reading a book) or to organise your ideas and see relationships between them.

11. Encourage your learners to think about their thinking

"Metacognition is the process of planning, assessing and monitoring one's own thinking." *Nisbet and Davies (1990)*

"If you really knew how your brain worked it would work much better." *Child quoted in Robert Fisher 'Teaching Thinking'*

There is a wealth of evidence to suggest that the more able and willing your learners are to think about their thinking, the better learners they will be and the more they will achieve. This is sometimes called metacognition and is thought of as the highest form of thinking, sitting above all the levels in Bloom's taxonomy (see Focus 7).

Metacognition is not easy and in the past it has been linked to intelligence and mental development. But we now know that young children can be reflective – they can and do think about their own thinking. As teachers we can help learners to develop it and to be aware of it. One way to do this is to extend the metaphor of the learning toolkit discussed in section 10 and think of metacognition as becoming aware that this toolkit exists, what tools are in it, which ones work best for you and when.

In 'Smart Schools' David Perkins (1992) asks how often are students asked to reflect on how they tackle maths problems? He points out that the teacher might build a discussion around questions like how do you begin? Do you read the problem more than once? Does that help? Does it help if you make a diagram? A table? A mental movie of what is happening in the 'story' of the problem? What helps for you?

It's important that teachers themselves are 'up-front' thinkers and learners. The teacher can model thought processes followed by hints and feedback to students about their performance. Good teachers talk with students about how they learn and continually ask questions that invite them to think about their own thinking. They stress that learning is a very personal thing, that we learn in different ways and that no one way is the best way *(see Different in Similar Ways).*

Developing metacognition requires that students have time and opportunity to talk to each other about thinking processes and make their own thought processes more explicit. Peer and self assessment both require and develop metacognition and many of the techniques associated with assessment for learning such as regular debriefing and learning logs support it *(see Assessment for Learning).*

11. Encourage your learners to think about their thinking

ENCOURAGE YOUR LEARNERS TO

think about
their thinking.

12. From a content to a learning curriculum

Despite the move towards teaching for understanding (see 'Teaching for Understanding: from coverage to comprehension') we still have a curriculum, especially secondary schools, that focuses too much on know-what and not enough on know-how. When we talk about continuity and progression we tend to think in terms of subjects and content rather than in terms of learning skills or developing minds.

We don't focus systematically enough on helping students to learn thinking skills and develop their minds. If we did we would be asking questions such as:

- When is this skill specifically taught as part of the course content and course aims?
- Where is this skill required and expected, but not explicitly taught as part of the course content and is not a specific aim of the course in itself?
- To what extent do teachers know what they can expect from their students generally and individually in terms of this skill at a particular age or stage? How do they know?
- To what extent is there continuity and progression in the way that this skill is used and developed across subjects and stages?

For some time now we in Learning Unlimited have been championing the idea of a learning curriculum based on a concept developed by Guy Claxton, namely the four R's of relevance, resilience, resourcefulness and reflectiveness. Claxton's 4 R's are really four 'selfs', namely self-motivation, self-confidence, self-reliance and self-awareness. We believe the curriculum should focus on the needs of young people first and society second. Being a smart thinker is not only about being a smart student or a smart worker, it's about being a smart citizen, a smart parent and smart friend as well.

The 4 selfs model was developed in partnership with Glasgow City Council who asked us to help them write a statement of principles to promote teaching for effective learning entitled 'Glasgow's for Learning' which was published in 2004. These four concepts are also closely mirrored in the recent statement from the Scottish Executive entitled 'Curriculum for Excellence'. In Scotland at least there seems to be a trend towards smart thinking. Who is setting it is not clear. Who should be setting it is, namely the teaching profession.

Relevance: self-motivation

Resilience: self-confidence

Resourcefulness: self-resilience

Reflectiveness: self-awareness

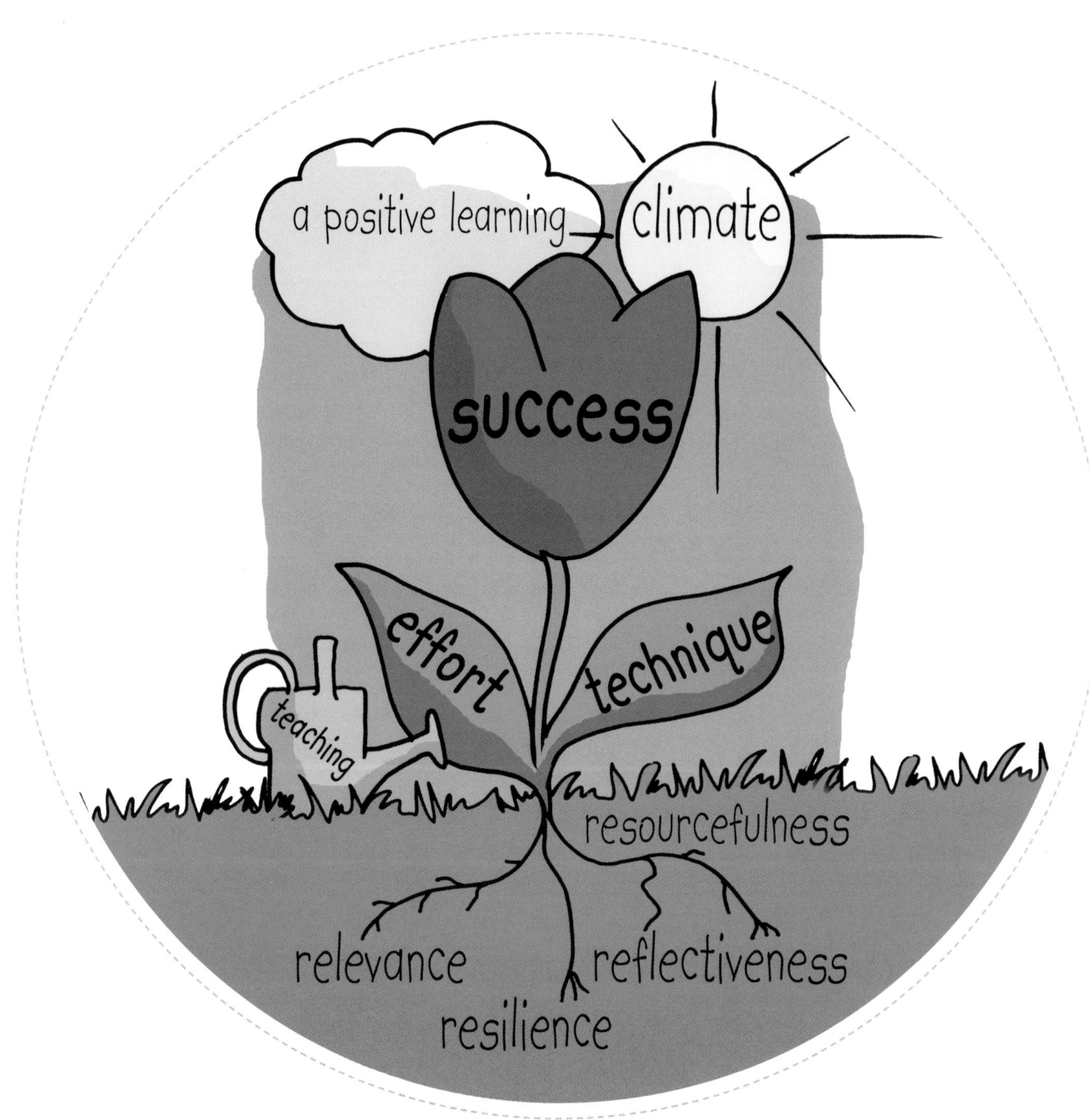

FROM CONTENT TO A
learning curriculum.

References and further reading

References

1. Carol McGuinness From Thinking Skills to Thinking Classrooms Research report no 115 DfEE, London, 1999.
2. Adey P and Shayler M 'Really Raising Standards: cognitive intervention and academic achievement' London Routledge, 1994.
3. Glasgow's for Learning, Glasgow City Council, 2004.
4. A Costa et al 'Developing Minds: A Resource Book for Teaching Thinking', ASCD, 2001.
5. David Perkins, 'Smart Schools', The Free Press, 1992.
6. Robert Sternberg and Louise Spear-Swerling, 'Teaching for Thinking', APA, 1996.
7. Valerie Wilson, SCRE 'Can Thinking Skills be Taught?' 2000.
8. John Nisbet, 'Teaching Thinking: an Introduction to the Research Literature', SCRE, 1990.
9. Guy Claxton 'Wise Up', Bloomsbury, London, 1999.
10. Philip Schlechty, 'Schools for the 21st Century', Jossey Bass, Oxford, 1991.
11. Watt Nicoll, 'Twisted Knickers and Stolen Scones', 1998.
12. Daniel Goleman 'Emotional Intelligence', Bantam Books, New York, 1995.
13. Howard Gardner, 'Frames of Mind', Harper Collins, London, 1983.
14. Steven Hastings, 'Thinking Skills', TES May 23rd, 2003.
15. Robin Fogarty et al, 'Teach for Transfer', Skylight Publishing, 1992.
16. Benjamin Bloom et al, 'A Taxonomy of Educational Objectives', 1956.
17. Magdalene Lampert, 'Teaching Problems and the Problems of Teaching', Yale, 2001.
18. Dewey 'How we think', 1933.
19. Guy Claxton, 'Building Learning Power', TLO Limited, Bristol, 2002.

Thinking programmes

1. Feuerstein R et al 'Instrumental Enrichment: an intervention for cognitive modifiability', Baltimore 1980.
2. The Somerset Thinking Skills Course: Handbook, Nigel Blagg et al, Basil Blackwell, 1988.
3. David Leat 'Thinking Through Geography', Chris Kington Publishers, Cambridge 1998.
   (Kington also publish thinking through various other subjects)
4. Edward De Bono's CoRT Thinking.
5. Let's Think: A Programme for Developing Thinking in Five and Six Year Olds, Philip Adey, Anne Robinson and Grady Venville. NFER Nelson.
6. A Guide to Better Thinking, Anne Kite, NFER Nelson.
7. Lipman M et al 'Philosophy in the Classroom', Philadelphia 1980.
8. Robert Fisher 'Teaching Thinking: Philosophical Enquiry in the Classroom', Cassell, London, 1998.

References and further reading continued

Further reading

1.   Robert Fisher 'Teaching Children to Think', Simon and Schuster, 1990.
2.   Robert Fisher 'Teaching Children to Learn', Stanley Thornes, 1995.
3.   Tony Buzan 'Use Your Head', BBC Books, 1982.
4.   Tony Buzan 'Make the Most of Your Mind', Simon and Schuster, 1977.
5.   Nancy Margulis 'Mapping Inner Space', Zephyr Press, Tucson Arizona.
6.   Karen Bromley et al, 'Graphic Organisers', Scholastic Press New York, 1995.
7.   Edward De Bono 'Six Thinking Hats', Penguin Books, 1985 and 'Six Thinking Hats for Schools', Perfect Learning Corporation, 1991.
8.   Oliver Caviglioni and Ian Harris 'Mapwise', Network Educational Press, Stafford 2000.
9.   Oliver Caviglioni, Ian Harris and Bill Tindall 'Eye Cue', Network Educational Press, Stafford 2002.
10. Edward De Bono 'De Bono's Thinking Course', BBC books, London, 1997.
11. Edward De Bono's Thinking Course, BBC Publications 1982.
12. Edward De Bono 'Teach your Child How to Think', Penguin 1992.

Websites

1.   www.edwdebono.com
2.   http://www.NFER-Nelson.co.uk
3.   www.case-network.org
4.   www.teachingthinking.net
5.   www.sapere.net
6.   www.criticalthinking.com